The Management Guide to Managing Yourself

Kate Keenan

GW00673704

Oval Books

Published by Oval Books
335 Kennington Road
London SE11 4QE
United Kingdom

Telephone: +44 (0)20 7582 7123
Fax: +44 (0)20 7582 1022
E-mail: info@ovalbooks.com

First published by Ravette Publishing, 1995
New edition published by Oval Books,1999

Series Editor – Anne Tauté
Editor – Catriona Scott

Cover designer – Jim Wire, Quantum
Printer – Cox & Wyman Ltd
Producer – Oval Projects Ltd

Cover – The difference between being
confused and being organised is how
well you manage yourself.

Acknowledgments and thanks to:
Barry Tuckwood
Jeremy Bethell
Angela Summerfield
Peggy Dalton

ISBN: 1-902825-76-4

Contents

This book is dedicated to
those who would like to manage better
but are too busy to begin.

Managing Yourself

Managing yourself is something that few people spend any time on at all. Life is not a dress rehearsal, and as far as it is known this is the only chance you get, so whether you work for a large enterprise, manage a household or run your own business, it is vital that you make the most of the opportunities which present themselves.

Most people want to do better in their endeavours. Those who achieve a measure of success are happy and productive. Managing yourself effectively is a key element in this process.

This book is about doing just that.

1. Juggling Your Life

Coping with life's demands is a constant juggling trick, and, like the juggler, most people have to keep a number of balls in the air at the same time.

There are three important areas where managing to do this is crucial – your work life, your home life and your personal life. The difficulty is that there is very rarely a time when all three areas are in harmony.

If you have two out of three under control at any one time, you are doing well. If two or more are presenting problems, you will probably find that you are spending most of your energy just coping. You will have very little time for yourself and certainly less time to take a look at how you are managing yourself.

Taking on Too Much

Most people take on too many responsibilities. Many of these are accepted willingly, but if you are a capable person more responsibilities may have been thrust on you because of your perceived ability to get things done. This means you probably have rather more to handle than you want.

What is worse, should you fail to achieve what other people require of you, they can be very unforgiving. This will feel very unfair as you are almost certainly doing more than most. Possibly you are not very good at saying no. Or perhaps you allow others to lean too much on you for support.

Taking on too much prevents you from managing yourself properly. You need to ask yourself if all your responsibilities are necessary: if they have been imposed upon you, or whether they have been self-created because this is what you think others expect of you. If so, you must decide what you are willing to take on and what you should jettison.

Being in a Rut

Working in a routine way can give you a false sense of security. You feel you are doing well because you are doing familiar things and you are so busy – too busy, perhaps, to make the active changes which could help you to manage yourself better.

You may have drifted into a situation and find yourself expected to carry out certain functions which were never formally agreed in the first place. Without realising it, you may have got into such a rut that it is quite impossible to see how firmly embedded you are.

Even if you do realise you are in a rut, the amount of effort you feel you would need in order to change your routine can appear daunting, especially if you are not sure what benefits you may achieve from doing so.

This is usually why it seems so much easier just to carry on as you are, instead of taking steps to do something about it.

Coping Badly

How well you are coping can be difficult to determine. Recognising that you may not be doing as well as you would like is the first step. Often a lack of personal organisation can be a symptom of the fact that you are coping badly. For instance:

- Frequently mislaying things.
- Not finding enough time to talk things through.
- Promising to do things and failing to deliver them.
- Finding that no amount of extra work makes any difference to the amount that remains.

If you recognise any of these, you need to work out how you might organise yourself better. Being well organised depends on how well you are managing yourself. But the common response to being under too much pressure is to feel that you have no time to get organised because you are so busy keeping up with what needs to be done. This is not a very productive approach, for if you do not organise yourself, you will never find it easy to get anything done. And the benefit of making an effort to get yourself organised is that you will be able to cope considerably better with whatever turns up.

The next step is to decide whether what you are doing is what you would like to be doing. Putting this into practice is more difficult, particularly if you have not sorted out which of your activities are necessary, which are self-imposed, and which have been thrust upon you.

Being Stressed

If you feel you are not managing yourself very well, you may be working under a good deal of stress without realising it. You may not even know that this is affecting you, nor understand why you feel things are constantly getting out of control.

Some stress is healthy. You need to be motivated to get out of bed and go to work. It is when your level of anxiety becomes so high you are prevented from getting things done that remedial action is required.

It may be that the goal posts have been moved. These could be within or without your work life – events over which you have no control. Having to do too many new things, dealing with increasing amounts of paperwork, electronic communications, etc. can also lead to stress. There are some warning signs which could indicate this:

- Always having to make excuses why things have not been done on time or are not to the agreed standard when previously this has not been a problem.

- Not undertaking extra things you would really like to do because you are feeling too tired.

- Being irritable and irascible about trivial things which usually do not bother you.

- Lacking enthusiasm for work which would normally spark your interest.

All these symptoms signal stress because they reflect behaviour that is out of the ordinary for you. You may be slow to realise that it is not work, but your own stress, that is the cause.

Seeking the Wrong Solutions

When trying to find ways of dealing with difficulties, some things which seem to be solutions can ultimately present you with other problems rather than permanent answers. You may recognise some of these:

- Blaming others or the circumstances. This is the usual method of averting guilt. You might even end up convincing yourself that it was not your fault.

- Ignoring things in the hope that if you do so for long enough, they will go away. Sadly this never happens; they simply get worse.

- Drinking alcohol as a way of blocking out the realities which are worrying you. This might make you feel better, but only for a short while. Then things seem just as bad as before, perhaps worse. The inevitable reaction is to have another drink.

- Eating junk food in an effort to comfort yourself. This cannot provide a substitute for what you crave and you only end up feeling worse since you now have the problem of extra pounds to contend with.

None of these are very sensible ways of managing. You may not notice that you have got into bad habits, nor that these seemingly attractive solutions only provide a temporary lift of spirits. Your situation will become more difficult in the long run since nothing, in fact, gets resolved.

Lacking a Sense of Direction

Having no objectives to work towards can be a major problem. If you lack a focus, or have no intermediate goal, you are not striving for a purpose but dealing with things as they crop up.

If you are not aiming for something specific you may find yourself caught like a hamster on a treadmill who keeps on running, but ultimately gets nowhere. In the beginning the exercise can be fun. But once you are running hell for leather, stopping has to be a conscious decision. You need to slow down and make a serious appraisal of where you are now and where you would like to be.

This could mean finding work more suitable for you. No-one should have to lead a life of quiet desperation. Even in an era of redundancy, there is always an alternative. Life is too short to continue to do work you detest.

But the unfamiliar is often scary simply because it is unfamiliar, so the temptation is to return to the well-trodden path, however much it lacks direction.

Summary: Facing Up To Things

If you recognise any of these symptoms, take a look at how you are managing yourself. There is no situation that cannot be improved. Nor is it ever the wrong time to start. You need not feel that "it's impossible", or "too late". Turning the clock back may not be an option, but when it slows down or stops, you can easily wind it up again.

Questions to Ask Yourself

Think about how you are managing yourself at the moment and answer the following questions:

◆ Am I finding it difficult to manage my home life, my personal life and my work life with equal success?

◆ Am I taking on too many responsibilities?

◆ Have I realised that I could be in a rut?

◆ Could routine activities be a way of avoiding making necessary changes?

◆ Am I finding it difficult to cope?

◆ Am I as well organised as I would like to be?

◆ Could I be suffering from high levels of stress?

◆ Have I slipped into some bad habits for coping with my problems?

If you have answered 'Yes' to some or all of these questions, your capacity to manage yourself probably requires some attention.

You'll Be Doing Better If...

★ You make an effort to ensure that at least two out of the three major areas of your life are satisfactory.

★ You acknowledge that you may have taken on too much.

★ You are prepared to find ways of improving your personal organisation.

★ You recognise that an effort is involved in getting out of your rut or off your treadmill.

★ You are more aware of some of your bad habits and are determined to eliminate them.

2. Understanding Yourself

Managing yourself involves understanding how you like to operate. If you are to get the maximum from your life and your work you need to understand how you prefer to function. This way you manage yourself properly and make sure that what you are doing is what you want to do.

Identifying your preferred approach to life is a key element in understanding yourself better. It enables you to evaluate the options open to you and to choose to do what would best suit you.

Working Out Your Preferences

Your preferences can be likened to handedness. If you write using, say, your right hand, the writing with that hand is practiced, easy and polished. This does not mean that you cannot use your left hand, but it does mean that your writing will be more laboured and you will require considerably more concentration than when writing with your preferred hand.

Knowing your preferences indicates the areas where you would be better to concentrate your efforts and those you are wisest to avoid if possible. It is useful to look at the options available. There are four basic sets of preferences:

- Organised or Spontaneous: how you react to life in general.
- Factual or Intuitive: how you prefer to take in information.
- Analytical or Sympathetic: how you prefer to process information and make decisions.
- Gregarious or Solitary: how you recharge your energy.

Organised or Spontaneous

This is about exploring your preferred life style. Think about which of the following statements applies to you:

☐ I prefer to have things organised, so that I know what I am doing most of the time.

☐ I prefer to do things on the spur of the moment; working in an orderly way cramps my style.

If you prefer to be organised, you will probably be happier working in situations which require planning and meeting schedules. You may become exasperated if you are required to face a dramatic change of course when something unexpected turns up.

If you prefer a more spontaneous way of doing things, you are likely to be happier working in more flexible, less structured situations. You could find working in a situation where things are routine and predetermined somewhat irksome.

This does not mean that you cannot function in your less preferred situation; simply that you will find it much harder to manage yourself.

Factual or Intuitive

How you absorb information plays an important part in the process of managing yourself. Think about how you prefer to gather and use information:

☐ I prefer to marshal all the facts and details; I am very good at recognising the practical realities of a situation.

☐ I prefer to look at the wider picture and explore possibilities; I like to work out different ways of doing things.

If you prefer to focus on all the facts available, you are unlikely to miss any important details which could affect the situation. But you have to watch that you do not spend so much time collecting these facts that opportunities pass you by.

If you prefer to look at the broader picture, you will want to explore all the possibilities and be interested in seeing meaning and patterns in the facts. Whilst this may produce creative insights, you could overlook a crucial detail, which could prevent a successful outcome.

You need to seek situations where your preferred way of processing information is productive. Working where your talents are not appreciated or where you are working against your preferences will result in frustration or worse still, exhaustion, as you will be using all your energies just coping with what is required.

For instance, if you take a factual approach, you may find that looking at the broad picture is woolly and lacking in substance, and working out a 5-year strategic plan might well defeat you. If you are intuitive, you may find that sticking to the facts restricts your creative processes, and that checking detailed lists is very hard work.

Analytical or Sympathetic

Everyone has to make decisions. Think about how you prefer to make them:

☐ I prefer to take an impartial and dispassionate approach which is based on logic.

☐ I prefer to take a compassionate and understanding approach which is based on seeing other people's points of view.

If you prefer to make decisions based on logic, you will probably be happier in a situation where objectivity and the ability to handle data and figures are a major requirement. If you take a more sympathetic approach, you will probably be more comfortable in situations where you can help or advise other people.

If you are analytical, you may be thought of as hard-hearted by those who take the softer approach. If you take a sympathetic stand, the analysts may see you as soft-hearted and sentimental.

Gregarious or Solitary

When you have run out of steam and need to regain your energy, think about how you would do this:

☐ I prefer doing something that involves people, such as going to a good party or visiting friends.

☐ I prefer spending time on my own, listening to music, reading or tinkering with a hobby.

If you prefer to be with people, working in a situation where you have little opportunity to exchange ideas with others could prove depressing. If you prefer to work quietly, coping with other people's constant demands could drive you to distraction.

Making Sense of Your Choices

By identifying how you prefer to behave in any given situation, you can begin to predict the circumstances where you are most likely to be successful.

- If you are Factual and Organised, you are likely to be a very responsible person who is most productive in situations which are precisely defined and where your carefulness and accuracy are valued.

- If you are Factual and Spontaneous, you will be very action-orientated and happier in situations where you can act as the troubleshooter and provide an immediate response to problems.

- If you are Intuitive and Analytical, you will always have lots of ideas and be more at home in situations where the overall objective has been identified and you can use your ingenuity to work to strategic goals.

- If you are Intuitive and Sympathetic, you will be very people-orientated and want to assist others to develop their potential to the full.

By studying the various combinations, it is apparent that people have different preferences on which they need to capitalise if they are to be at their most productive.

Realising how you prefer to do things can be useful.

It is also worth comparing your views with someone whose perspective is the opposite of yours. That way, you get the benefits of both processes.

Understanding your personal preferences helps you to seek the kind of job in which your assets can be used to best advantage. It also helps you to avoid occupations where you could be required to work against your preferences. If you have to work in such a situation you will find it takes a great deal of energy just to stay still; you can become burnt out and disillusioned in the attempt.

So try not to go with choices that are fiendishly difficult; instead go with your natural inclinations.

Summary: Assessing Yourself

Being aware of what you are good at is not the same thing as wanting to be good at something; so beware of chasing shadows. The process of assessing yourself may require some soul-searching, especially if you have never given much thought to it before.

Examining your preferences provides you with enough self-knowledge to take the right decisions about the kind of work which would be most fulfilling for you and this, in turn, enables you to make the most of yourself.

Questions to Ask Yourself

Think about how you prefer to perceive and assess the world around you and answer the following questions:

♦ Can I identify my preferred ways of approaching life?

♦ Am I more aware of how my preferences influence my life?

♦ Do I know how I prefer to manage my life?

♦ Do I know how I prefer to take in information?

♦ Do I know how I prefer to tackle problems and make decisions?

♦ Can I identify the sorts of activities it would be best for me to avoid?

♦ Can I identify the sorts of circumstances in which I would be likely to work more productively?

You'll Be Doing Better If...

★ You identify the ways you prefer to function.

★ You have an insight into what sort of activities would suit you best.

★ You appreciate how you prefer to process information when making decisions.

★ You realise that there are other ways to view things which have as much validity as your own.

★ You are able to use your preferences to seek the situation that will suit you best.

★ You make the right choices for yourself.

3. Being Effective

Managing yourself effectively requires you to decide what you want to achieve. This means being single-minded in defining your goals and determining what you do. It stops you from taking on impossible tasks and ensures that you concentrate your efforts to best effect.

Taking Stock

To manage yourself properly, you have to take stock of your current situation, and identify the demands and expectations being made on you and your time, both personally and professionally.

Think about your current situation and make a list of the major activities you carry out. Then review your list and single out:

- Those activities you enjoy doing.
- Those activities you would like to do more of.
- Those activities you would like to do less of.

By doing this you are able to take stock of what you would like to keep doing and what you would like to change, which makes it much easier to decide the direction you want to take.

Deciding Your Direction

If you are not to find yourself simply falling in with whatever happens at the time, you have to draw a line across your life and decide what you want to do.

It is said that 'life is what happens to you while you are busy making other plans'. Implementing short-term personal plans, such as decorating a house or buying a car, usually takes up considerable time and energy. Longer-term (and more important) plans, such as making a radical career move or setting up a new business, tend to be allocated less time and are often implemented on the principle that 'it seemed a good idea at the time'.

Deciding your direction deserves a structured approach. Think about what you would like to achieve and make a list of what you want from two areas:

- **Your personal life**: what you need from your relationships with friends, family and colleagues.

- **Your work life**: what you would like to accomplish in your career, and in what other directions you could develop.

When you have worked out what you want, think about how easy or difficult it will be for you to achieve the three most important things on your list.

If they are all difficult to accomplish, you may have set yourself unrealistic objectives. Add a few reasonable aims. If you can achieve some things with a moderate amount of effort in a reasonable timescale, you will feel that you are more in control of your life.

To prevent yourself from going in the wrong direction you need to have a broad idea of what you want from your life and where you want it to go, and keep your chosen aims in view.

Limiting Your Responsibilities

People who manage themselves well are usually clear about one central aspect of how they manage their activities: they know the areas they are prepared to accept responsibility for. This stops them dissipating their efforts on activities which undermine their personal effectiveness.

By recognising how your efforts fit into the wider perspective, you are able to see where you may have been going badly adrift, happily making work for yourself unnecessarily, or causing yourself problems because you find it difficult to limit the scope of what it is you are responsible for.

Just because you are answerable for results does not necessarily mean that you need to get involved with the day-to-day details. If you regard every single thing for which you feel responsible as something you must do yourself, you will inevitably find yourself overwhelmed.

Separate the responsibilities you are willing to take on from those you are no longer prepared to undertake. Then take steps to get rid of the unwanted ones.

Adapting to Change

Few things in life stay static but you cannot get far by behaving like an ostrich and sticking your head in the sand in the hope that if you do not face up to change, it will not happen. Being willing to adapt is an important part of managing yourself.

Dealing with change is often a frightening experience because the outcome is unsure and risk is usually involved. But if you are not able to cope with changes, you will eventually fall far behind those who are. Remember, it is easier to keep up, than to catch up.

Having a strategy to implement change helps you not only to maintain the status quo, but to keep your end up when everyone about you seems to be moving forward. Fortunately, it is not that difficult. You can meet change in three basic ways:

1. Enlarging your skills by going on courses, learning new techniques and trying out different things.

2. Adding to your knowledge by keeping abreast of the latest information and actively finding out about new developments.

3. Adapting your attitudes by keeping an open mind and changing it when you see that a new way of doing something is better.

If you can develop your knowledge and skills, you will become less resistant to coping with change. By being less afraid of change, you will become more receptive to new ideas and situations.

Being Organised

If you are serious about managing yourself you need to know where things are, and access them without difficulty. Nothing is more frustrating than being stranded on some far-flung station platform with the correct change but the old telephone number.

Personal organisation is easily achieved by:

- Using your diary as a record system for information, for listing the things you need to do, and for logging things that happen as you go along. This means you will never again have to experience the exasperation of searching for notes on the backs of envelopes.

- Being tidy. This enables you to find things quickly and makes you feel efficient.

- Keeping things together that belong together. This saves you time and gives you a sensation of being in control. To be able to find what you want without having to rummage through everything first is an obvious advantage.

- Having a regular clear-out. This often exposes things that have gone astray and is a most fulfilling exercise in itself.

- Clearing your desk by the end of the day. This indicates that you have dealt with your tasks and is immensely satisfying. It allows you to start afresh the next day, with nothing left over to clear up.

- Keeping a reserve stock of essentials. This prevents you from running out of some vital commodity when time is at a premium. Making it your business to buy another before the first runs out means you are never caught in a crisis due to lack of forethought.

- Making daily check lists and ticking off items as they are done. When you are really busy you should not be cluttering your memory with short-term trivia. This means you do not have to re-check that something needs to be checked just because you cannot recall if you checked it in the first place.

- Having a permanent check list for regular activities, such as the items to pack when travelling. This means that instead of forgetting something indispensable, you can check things off your master list each time.

Even if you are congenitally untidy, it should be possible to enact one or more of these simple methods to keep on top of everyday activities. Being organised stops you getting fraught and tangled up in irrelevant issues and keeps you functioning productively.

Summary: Being in Control

To manage yourself properly you have to find the time and energy to determine your direction and decide what you want. Once you have decided what is important to you, you have to take stock of what you are doing and whether this is what you ought to be doing and whether you need to do it all yourself.

Being organised prevents you from being deflected from the main task and adapting to change ensures that you keep up-to-date.

Jettisoning unnecessary responsibility stops you becoming overloaded. Limiting yourself means that you liberate yourself. It gives you the freedom to do what you should be doing.

Questions to Ask Yourself

Think about how effective you are personally and answer the following questions:

♦ Have I taken stock of my current situation?

♦ Am I clear about my direction?

♦ Have I listed what I want to achieve?

♦ Have I identified which responsibilities I am prepared to meet and which I need to get rid of?

♦ Am I making an effort to keep up-to-date by improving my knowledge and skills?

♦ Am I striving to keep an open-minded attitude to changes?

♦ Am I better organised and more able to find things at a moment's notice?

♦ Am I feeling more effective?

You Will Be Doing Better If...

★ You take stock.

★ You know what you would like to change.

★ You have a good idea of your direction.

★ You list what you would like to achieve in your work and personal life.

★ You concentrate on what you want to do and not let anything deflect you.

★ You limit your responsibilities.

★ You add to your knowledge and enlarge your skills.

★ You are much more open-minded about change.

★ You are relatively well-organised so that you can focus on getting things done.

★ You feel you are being more effective.

4.   Taking Charge

To manage yourself, you need to take charge of yourself and make things happen. There are a number of things you have to do to bring this about.

Valuing Yourself

How you view yourself is an important ingredient in your ability to take charge. If you do not rate yourself very highly, you may not think it is worth putting any effort into managing yourself. And if you do not value yourself, how can you expect others to do so?

Make a list of what you like about yourself and what you do not like. You will find that what you like are those things which give you confidence. What you do not like you can either accept as part of the package, or decide to do something about.

Your opinion of yourself is the only one that matters but if it is to be a good one, you have to earn it. No amount of praise from others can make you value yourself if you do not feel worthwhile. You may also discount other people's praise because you feel that you do not deserve it.

The achievement of something which makes you feel good about yourself need not be enormous. Start with fairly simple standards, things you can achieve and measure easily, such as:

- Making a point of turning up on time.

- Completing things within deadlines.

- Doing what you say you will do.

- Getting one thing done that you do not want to do.

- Finishing something that you started and never completed.

By living up to the standards that you set yourself, you will not only earn your own self-respect, but maintain it.

Once you are achieving these things, the validation (or corroboration) you receive from other people who appreciate your efforts also becomes a reward, and you will be able to give their praise credence because you know you have earned it.

It is important to remember that no-one can make you feel inferior without your consent. Valuing yourself gives you a sense of self-worth which boosts your confidence and enables you to achieve more.

Asserting Yourself

There are two things people find hard to do because they involve imposing their will on others:

1. Getting Your Own Way

Asking for what you want in order to get your own way is not always easy, usually because you fear a refusal. Being refused is always possible and you need to accept the fact and not be upset by it.

How you express what you want can make all a difference, e.g. "Wouldn't it be a good idea if...?" is rather more effective than "I want..." Or, "I know you are busy, but I did ask you to..." will achieve more than "Why haven't you done what I asked?"

If you are not used to getting your own way, and then you get it, it can be spoiled by feelings of guilt. You need not feel guilty that you have got what you asked for. Accept it as if it were your right. More often than not, it is.

2. Saying No

Saying 'No' to other people can be a major problem. To reduce the number of times you have to do so, ask yourself why you are the one who gets such requests from others. It may be because you are a nice person or it could be that others see you as 'soft' – one who will bale them out of difficulties they should never have got into in the first place.

Possibly you are so conscientious that you always manage to get everything done – sometimes at an unacceptable personal cost. Or perhaps other people are simply more insistent and/or selfish than you are.

Examine the amount of help you usually give. If you take over a task, you use up your own valuable time. Try indicating where information can be obtained and leaving people to work out how to do the rest.

This strategy has two main advantages:

- You do not have to do it yourself.

- Others learn how to do things through their own efforts with limited guidance. They will not need to ask you again – at least about that concern.

The usual reasons why it is difficult to say 'No' are that you feel it will make you unpopular or that you are pressurised into doing something before you can think clearly enough to refuse.

But saying 'No' does not make you unpopular provided you do it constructively by offering advice to help others solve their own problems. If you keep a ready phrase in mind for use when declining a request in a calm, steady tone of voice (e.g. "No, I can't help you with that, but what I suggest is…"), you will not be press-ganged into doing something you would rather not do.

When refusing something you do not want to do, you simply repeat your refusal like a broken record until the other person gives in and accepts your response: "I already have a commitment that night", "I'm just not available that evening"; and so on.

Allowing others to walk all over you only encourages them to do so time and again. You can prevent yourself from being dumped upon if you show each would-be dumper that you are no longer prepared to be the dumping ground.

By responding in a firm but unaggressive manner you will find it happening less and less, mainly because you have shown that you value your time and therefore yourself. People who value themselves are valued by others.

Being Persistent

Once you have made a decision, you need to see it through. This is where sheer determination becomes a major virtue. It is often not the most brilliant people who are the most successful, but the ones who plug away day after day and achieve spectacular results by sheer perseverance.

Of course, you must be one hundred per cent convinced that what you are doing is the right thing for you. Even when this is the case, there may be obstacles to prevent you from making it happen, not least other people. Others can be very good at pointing out all the negative aspects of your intended course of action. They can think of endless reasons why something will not work, but are much less good at encouraging you.

This is why you usually have to rely on yourself, and the quality of persistence is one which you need to develop and nurture. You can achieve great things against all odds if you believe in something enough to keep at it and never give up. Always remember that it was the tortoise who won the race.

Coping with Stress

Primitive peoples were 'hunter-gatherers' keeping themselves and their tribes alive by hunting wild animals, fighting others, and struggling to exist. It was a life that involved fear and anger by turns.

Being angry or frightened is still part of the human condition and the body is designed to allow you to cope with it. Your system reacts by preparing you either for:

- Fight – if you are brave enough or angry enough to stand up for yourself (or do not have a way of escaping); or for

- Flight – if you judge it would be wiser to get away from a threatening situation.

When you feel stressed, it is one or other (sometimes both) of these emotions which are triggered. The problem is that, in most current situations, the options for fight or for flight are not viable, but the human system will have readied itself to enact one or the other. The energy is pent up. It has nowhere to go. This is why you feel stressed.

The remedy is also physical. Putting the body and mind to work by involving them in activities of the 'fight or flight' kind reduces the stress. There are three excellent ways of doing this, namely:

- Engaging in physical activity. This puts your body back into a balanced and normal state and thereby reduces tension.

- Talking and socialising. This releases your pent-up energy by being with people, laughing and talking.

- Planning and making lists. This is a less active way of coping, but one which nonetheless uses intellectual energy.

All three methods work but it is the combination that produces the best results.

Expending physical energy may seem to be an extreme solution for alleviating stress. But you do not need to change your life style radically. Simply add an activity to your daily routine which helps you release pent-up energy, such as:

- Taking a brisk walk – even if it is only getting off the bus a few stops sooner than you need to.

- Swimming – a soothing form of exercise which allows you to do as much as you feel able to.

- Working out at a gym or at home with a videotape – which can mean an improved figure and tone-up, as well as a release from pressure.

There are other activities which the more competitive will be attracted to, such as tennis, squash, etc. The message is to tailor your exercise to your interests and way of life.

However small the activity, the effects are immediate. Even if you start reluctantly, you will find it quickly becomes a welcome ritual, and that if a day passes by when a brisk walk is not possible, you will feel restless and tense. Taking some form of exercise clears the body and mind of unwanted energy and negative emotions.

Summary: Knowing What to Do

Having a good opinion of yourself, knowing how to get what you want without feeling guilty or upsetting people, being persistent when you want to achieve things and taking action to rid yourself of stress enables you to take charge of yourself and to get the things done that you want to do.

Questions to Ask Yourself

Think about whether you are taking charge of yourself and answer the following questions:

♦ Am I valuing myself?

♦ Am I asking for what I want?

♦ Am I prepared to say 'No' to requests?

♦ Am I determined to keep plugging away in order to achieve what I want?

♦ Am I working actively and systematically to reduce my stress levels?

♦ Am I feeling more in charge of myself?

You Will Be Doing Better If...

★ You enhance your self-esteem.

★ You state clearly what you want.

★ You say 'No' calmly and confidently.

★ You persevere in your efforts to achieve what you want, despite all odds.

★ You use the method of reducing stress which works best for you.

★ You feel that things are going your way.

5. Getting on with Others

Most activities involve you working in some way or another with people. Whatever you do – whether you work with equipment, supervise staff, manage a family, or work on your own – you need to deal with others to achieve your objectives. How you get on with them will make a difference to managing yourself.

Getting on well with people is a skill which some people seem to be more successful at than others. But there is one way of making sure that you do well enough for all intents and purposes. The trick is to remember that you are the constant factor which affects the outcome of all your dealings with people.

A major step towards improving your relationships with people is to assess how you may be viewing them.

Your Behaviour Towards Others

Everyone has an attitude towards the people with whom they come into contact. They also have an attitude about themselves. Both together colour the way they behave.

In simplistic terms, you can view yourself as:

- A decent, honest person trying to make the best of all that comes your way. (I'm all right.)

- An unlucky person, someone who never wins the raffle. (I'm not all right.)

And you can see others as:

- People who are decent, honest and trying to do the same as you. (They're all right.)

- People who are not capable of being trusted and who will usually let you down. (They're not all right.)

From this analysis four combinations are apparent. They are worth exploring as they shed light on the way you get on with others.

1. **'I'm not all right – They're all right.'** People who believe this feel they are not much good at anything and that they get most things wrong. They feel other people are usually luckier and cleverer than they are. These people may take things too much to heart or be wasting energy on envy.

2. **'I'm not all right – They're not all right.'** People who believe this feel they are not much good at anything and that the rest of the world is pretty useless too. These people tend not to care about themselves or what others think of them. Nor do they care about others.

3. **'I'm all right – They're not all right**.' Those who believe this feel that, while they know what is going on in their life and how to handle things, other people are stupid or worthless. These people can be arrogant and intimidating and put people down by constantly denigrating and patronising them.

4. **'I'm all right – They're all right**.' These people feel good about themselves and are able to do things well. They also feel that most other people are likable, decent human beings. Because these people feel good about themselves and other people, they are able to handle awkward situations more easily. They can see that even the most difficult person has a story to tell which would explain their behaviour. They can distinguish between bad behaviour and a bad person.

You Have a Choice

It is fairly obvious that the most constructive attitude when it comes to getting on with other people is the 'I'm all right – They're all right' option. This position offers mutual respect and a positive approach to making relationships productive.

You might ask why people do not always adopt this attitude. It seems strange to assume anything less than the optimum position for achieving good relations.

But when you have a bad day or things get you down, there is a tendency to slide into one of the other attitudes. Which one you adopt will very often reflect your past experiences, or what is happening in your life at the time.

The main thing to realise is that when this happens, you always have a choice to change your perspective on life and your view of others. You can choose to be 'all right' and choose to think that the people you are dealing with are also 'all right', but that perhaps they are having a bad day or have made an understandable mistake.

By recognising that you have a choice, you put yourself in control and being in control means that you are managing yourself, rather than letting situations overcome you.

The Power of Your Behaviour

It is only through your behaviour that people can judge you as a person since it is this which indicates to them what is going on in your mind and how you are feeling.

It is important to be aware that the way you behave will usually prompt similar behaviour in others. Like a pebble thrown into a pond, the ripples extend outwards from the impact and have an influence to a greater extent than you would credit.

In simplistic terms, if you are pleasant and polite most people tend to respond to you in like manner. Conversely, if you are grumpy and dispirited, you should not be surprised if people react to you in the same way.

You might feel this is obvious – a simple matter of 'Do as you would be done by' – but unless you constantly remind yourself of this maxim you may forget that your behaviour can have infinite repercussions.

Summary: Managing Your Behaviour

To have good relations with other people you need to exert some control over yourself. By choosing how you view other people, you are in fact determining how you will behave towards them.

The way you behave towards others has a direct effect on the way they respond to you. It is important to be aware of the power of your behaviour and its influence on your relationships.

Questions to Ask Yourself

Think about your dealings with people and answer the following questions:

♦ Do I need to improve my relationships with people?

♦ Am I aware of the different approaches that can be taken?

♦ Do I consistently choose an 'I'm all right – They're all right' approach?

♦ Am I aware of the effect that others people's behaviour can have on me?

♦ Am I conscious of the influence my behaviour can have on the way others respond?

You'll Be Doing Better If...

★ You appreciate the ways in which people can view themselves and others.

★ You evaluate your outlook and decide whether you need to take action.

★ You make a conscious effort to choose an 'I'm all right – They're all right' approach.

★ You understand the power of your behaviour.

★ You find that working with other people is easier and more productive.

6.   Living Positively

Having a philosophy which brings a sense of well-being determines a great deal about the way you manage yourself. There are several ways to achieve this, and all of them relate to your attitude to life.

Being Positive

You can decide how you think. If you choose to think positively you can clear out a lot of unwanted emotions which may be blocking you from making the best of yourself. For instance, you can:

- Keep calm. If you let others anger you they have won. Count to three before you respond. It stops you from being provoked into saying what you would not say when rational.

- Put things behind you. If you let yourself think about getting your own back on someone who has caused you grief, it only allows the person who hurt you to hurt you longer. Think of something else when you find your thoughts heading in that direction. Eventually you will not have to.

- Find merit. If you dislike something or someone, find the one thing you do like (there is usually one) and focus on that.

- Be cheerful. If you find it difficult, act it. In a very short time you will find it is no longer an act.

- Think of problems as challenges or opportunities and act accordingly. This way you will find it possible to achieve positive results.

If you can develop hardy attitudes, like a plant which withstands the frost, you will find it a great deal easier to cope with what life brings. You can do this by taking positive action. For example:

- If you are feeling depressed, read a book, play an instrument, telephone someone. Concentrating on something other than yourself makes it impossible to dwell on your problems.

- Smiling. It is a rare person who does not respond to a smile. Not only will your feelings be reinforced by their friendly reactions but when you smile your brain activates endorphins, the body's natural pain relieving system, so you end up feeling even better yourself.

- If you have no suitable support from friends or family, find a qualified therapist. It can be rewarding and revealing to talk to a neutral party about very personal things. A good therapist will help you to make a plan of action and institute a time-frame for you to sort yourself out.

Looking After Yourself

If you are to manage yourself positively, looking after yourself is an important part of the process. It is all very well gaining in-depth self-knowledge, but if you have no energy, you may be wasting your time.

The first question to ask yourself when it comes to your personal well-being is, "Where am I in the queue for attention?" The answer is likely to be, "At the back."

You probably have a great many things to attend to which take precedence over paying attention to yourself. But given these obligations, there is all the more need to look after yourself. Learn to pamper yourself. There are a number of instant and effective ways:

- Run a deep bath, put on some soothing music, place candles around the bathroom, sprinkle something aromatic into the water – then lie in the bath, in the candlelight, and relax.
- Book yourself a massage with a masseuse, an aromatherapist or a reflexologist.
- Take yourself off for a 2-day break at a health farm or go sailing, ski-ing, hill-walking, riding, gliding.
- Meet a friend at a luxury venue for breakfast or drinks; neither of which need be very expensive.
- Take time off to indulge yourself in something, anything, that you just love doing.

Leading a Balanced Life

The old adage relating to all work and no play is particularly relevant to managing yourself effectively. When you work hard and consistently, you need to give yourself permission to take time off.

If you allocate time to enjoy your social and family life, you will not get stale at work, nor will you resent long working hours with no let-up. The balance brings benefits to both worlds. By making the effort to separate work from pleasure you will feel in control of your life, rather than dominated by it.

Realising Your Dreams

Having pipe dreams gives you a way of expressing yourself. They transport you from a more mundane existence into the fantasy world of what you would really like to happen. Instead of suppressing dreams you can go some way towards realising them by not waiting for the day when you can afford or have time to achieve them.

Write down what you would really like to do, assuming you had no responsibilities. For example, you may hanker after the life style that encompasses sipping Martinis under a parasol on a tropical island or you may crave the thrill of driving a Formula One racing car. While both these ambitions seem to be out of range for most people, with a bit of effort and a modicum of imagination, achieving part of them may not be as outlandish as it first appears.

For instance, you could set up a deck chair and garden umbrella in the back yard, mix your own exotic cocktail, and by emulating the image of your dream, enjoy the moment. Or to simulate the exhilaration of going at speed, you could take a ride on a roller-coaster, or take up white water racing at weekends. To fulfil the longing for the experience, the secret is to get as close to it as possible.

Happy and fulfilled people are those who do something positive about meeting their needs now, on however small a scale, instead of yearning for what is currently unobtainable. It is amazing, with a bit of lateral thinking and determination, how nearly you can come to realising your dreams.

Summary: Feeling Good

The ultimate goal of managing yourself is to feel good and achieve what you want. Always remember that you have a choice. If you are not feeling good about yourself, this could also be by your own choice. So be sure you choose positive attitudes, the ones which determine your success.

Questions to Ask Yourself

Think about whether you are taking a positive attitude to your life and answer the following questions:

♦ Am I making an effort to control my emotions?

♦ Am I putting bad experiences behind me?

♦ Am I controlling negative thoughts by taking positive action?

♦ Have I developed hardy attitudes?

♦ Am I smiling enough?

♦ Am I looking after myself and treating myself on occasions?

♦ Am I successfully balancing my home life and work life?

♦ Have I devised a way to come close to achieving my pipe-dreams?

♦ Am I managing to achieve a sense of well-being?

You Will Be Doing Better If...

★ You are more in control of your emotions.

★ You develop hardier attitudes.

★ You feel better because you are smiling more.

★ You take time to relax and do interesting things.

★ You maintain a balance between your work and your personal relationships.

★ You nurture a sense of well-being.

★ You achieve some of the things you most wish for.

Check List for Managing Yourself

If you are finding that managing yourself is proving to be more difficult than you thought, think about whether it is because you have failed to take account of one or more of the following aspects:

Understanding Yourself

If you have not taken time to analyse how you like to operate, you may not have identified your preferences. This means that you may be working against the grain or running hard just to stay still. Or you may have identified your preferences but not worked out what it means for you. Knowing the type of activities where you would be best to concentrate your efforts helps you to choose the right occupation.

Having Direction

If you have not decided what you want from your life, you will almost certainly find yourself going in the wrong direction. It may be that you have not yet taken stock of your situation or chosen which responsibilities you are prepared to shoulder and which ones to reject. Possibly you are not very well organised or you may be resisting change. In any event, you are not on track or in full control.

Taking Charge

If you are finding taking charge is still a problem, it could be that you are not asserting yourself and are still letting the needs of others take priority over your own desires. It may be that you do not value yourself enough because you have not earned you own self-esteem or because you are not persistent enough. But most of all, you may not yet have got round to taking some form of exercise to rid yourself of stress.

Getting on With People

If you find you are not getting on very well with others, it may be that your attitude towards them or your attitude towards yourself is less than positive. If you are not choosing a constructive approach you will inevitably find others are less helpful. If you have not fully appreciated the power your behaviour has in determining that of others, you may not realise how much it can influence other people's attitudes towards you.

Living Positively

If you do not have a sense of well-being, you may not be looking after yourself properly. If you are not leading a balanced life, you will find it difficult to work well. Doing something you have always wanted will bring you some measure of content.

The Benefits of Managing Yourself

Taking time to understand yourself better is important. If you do not manage yourself, you will find achieving your potential less easy and you will not be as successful as you want to be and expect to be.

Think about how you spend most days. On average, you will usually be spending:

- 8 hours or so asleep.

- 8 hours or more at work.

- 2 hours or so squandered (travelling, queuing, waiting for telephone calls, etc.).

- 2-4 hours eating.

- 4-6 hours or less for leisure and pleasure.

It is important that you make the best of your waking hours, otherwise you end up wasting your life. Not managing yourself means that you let things manage you, rather than taking control of them.

Just wanting something to happen is not going to make it happen. You are the only person who can determine what you think and how you want to behave. You have the ability to think positively and reap the benefits. Manage yourself well and you will make the most of your life and get the best out of it.

Glossary

Here are some definitions relating to Managing Yourself.

Assertion – Expression of needs in a non-threatening manner; not to be confused with aggression.

Attitude – Frame of mind which can be altered at will.

Behaviour – Actions which you can choose to control.

Changes – Disturbances which need to be embraced as opportunities.

Demands – The unremitting expectations of others.

Direction – The way forward which needs to be purposeful rather than haphazard.

Goal – A focus for effort.

Lists – Life-lines to being organised.

Pipe dreams – Fantasies which, with a bit of ingenuity, can become realities.

Preferences – Natural inclinations to choose some things over others.

Responsibilities – Obligations which need radical periodic pruning.

Rut – A familiar track which leads nowhere.

Stress – A negative mental state which needs positive action to alleviate.

Validation – Authentication of self-esteem; only meaningful once you feel you have earned it.

Self-Managing Concepts

There are two famous forms of self-analysis which assist people in managing themselves:

Myers-Briggs Type Indicator – A questionnaire which, when completed and analysed, is used to help people understand their preferences, and then integrate that understanding into their lives.

Transactional Analysis – Eric Berne's philosophy which includes the concept that life positions have a direct bearing on relationships and interactions with others; subsequently expressed as 'I'm O.K. – You're O.K.' by Thomas Harris.

The Author

Kate Keenan is a Chartered Occupational Psychologist with degrees in affiliated subjects (B.Sc., M.Phil.) and a number of qualifications in others.

She founded Keenan Research, an industrial psychology consultancy, in 1978. The work of the consultancy is fundamentally concerned with helping people to achieve their potential and make a better job of their management.

By devising work programmes for companies she enables them to target and remedy their managerial problems – from personnel selection and individual assessment to team building and attitude surveys. She believes in giving priority to training the managers to institute their own programmes, so that their company resources are developed and expanded.

Having long believed that the key to being successful in management is to be good at managing yourself she is constantly inspired by others who do so even better than she does.

THE MANAGEMENT GUIDES

'Especially for people who have neither the time nor the inclination for ploughing through the normal tomes...'

The Daily Telegraph

Asserting Yourself

Delegating

Handling Stress

Making Time

Managing

Managing Yourself

Motivating

Negotiating

Planning

Running Meetings

Selecting People

Understanding Behaviour

These books are available from your local bookshop in the UK, or from the publishers:

Oval Books, 335 Kennington Road, London SE11 4QE
Telephone: (0) 20 7582 7123; Fax: (0) 20 7582 4887;
E-mail: info@ovalbooks.com

The Management Guides are also available from the publishers on audio cassette, and in electronic form for PDAs.